In 1935 if you wanted to
read a good book, you needed
either a lot of money or a library card.
Cheap paperbacks were available, but their
poor production generally mirrored the quality
between the covers. One weekend that year,
Allen Lane, Managing Director of The Bodley Head,
having spent the weekend visiting Agatha Christie,
found himself on a platform at Exeter station trying to
find something to read for his journey back to London.
He was appalled by the quality of the material he had to
choose from. Everything that Allen Lane achieved from that
day until his death in 1970 was based on a passionate belief
in the existence of 'a vast reading public for *intelligent*
books at a low price'. The result of his momentous vision
was the birth not only of Penguin, but of the 'paperback
revolution'. Quality writing became available for the price of
a packet of cigarettes, literature became a mass medium
for the first time, a nation of book-borrowers became a
nation of book-buyers – and the very concept of book
publishing was changed for ever. Those founding
principles – of quality and value, with an overarching
belief in the fundamental importance of reading –
have guided everything the company has
done since 1935. Sir Allen Lane's
pioneering spirit is still very much alive
at Penguin in 2005. Here's to
the next 70 years!

MORE THAN A BUSINESS

'We decided it was time to end the almost customary half-hearted manner in which cheap editions were produced – as though the only people who could possibly want cheap editions must belong to a lower order of intelligence. We, however, believed in the existence in this country of a vast reading public for intelligent books at a low price, and staked everything on it'
Sir Allen Lane, 1902–1970

'The Penguin Books are splendid value for sixpence, so splendid that if other publishers had any sense they would combine against them and suppress them'
George Orwell

'More than a business ... a national cultural asset'
Guardian

'When you look at the whole Penguin achievement you know that it constitutes, in action, one of the more democratic successes of our recent social history'
Richard Hoggart

The Assault on Jerusalem

STEVEN RUNCIMAN

PENGUIN BOOKS

PENGUIN BOOKS

Published by the Penguin Group
Penguin Books Ltd, 80 Strand, London WC2R 0RL, England
Penguin Group (USA) Inc., 375 Hudson Street, New York, New York 10014, USA
Penguin Group (Canada), 10 Alcorn Avenue, Toronto, Ontario, Canada M4V 3B2
(a division of Pearson Penguin Canada Inc.)
Penguin Ireland, 25 St Stephen's Green, Dublin 2, Ireland
(a division of Penguin Books Ltd)
Penguin Group (Australia), 250 Camberwell Road, Camberwell, Victoria 3124,
Australia (a division of Pearson Australia Group Pty Ltd)
Penguin Books India Pvt Ltd, 11 Community Centre,
Panchsheel Park, New Delhi – 110 017, India
Penguin Group (NZ), cnr Airborne and Rosedale Roads, Albany,
Auckland 1310, New Zealand (a division of Pearson New Zealand Ltd)
Penguin Books (South Africa) (Pty) Ltd, 24 Sturdee Avenue,
Rosebank 2196, South Africa

Penguin Books Ltd, Registered Offices: 80 Strand, London WC2R 0RL, England

www.penguin.com

A History of the Crusades: Volume I first published by
Cambridge University Press 1951
Published in Penguin Books 1965
This extract published as a Pocket Penguin 2005

1

Copyright 1951 by Cambridge University Press
All rights reserved

Set in 11.5/13.5pt Monotype Dante
Typeset by Palimpsest Book Production Limited
Polmont, Stirlingshire
Printed in England by Clays Ltd, St Ives plc

Contents

Publisher's Note

The Crusades were the attempt by Western and Central Europeans to subjugate the Moslem Middle East and carve out Christian colonies in the lands associated with the Bible. They also came to stand for a variety of other military projects against 'pagans' or Christian 'heretics'. The Christian Byzantine Empire centred on Constantinople (Istanbul) had traditionally been the bulwark against Islam in the East and had, as *The Assault on Jerusalem* makes clear, an awkward role in the Crusades: notionally a beneficiary of European help but in practice compromised and undermined. The Crusades remain one of the most contentious and disturbing subjects in the history of the Mediterranean and have been a subject of polemic between Christians and Moslems now for some nine hundred years.

In these extracts from Steven Runciman's marvellous three-volume history of the Crusades, some of the key events of the First Crusade are dramatized: the Pope's astonishing call to arms that launched the crusading movement in 1095, the catastrophic People's Crusade and two of the military climaxes of the successful campaign (a success never really matched by later crusades): the siege and capture of Nicaea (now called Iznik) and of Jerusalem: the ultimate military and religious goal. The massacre that accompanied the latter's capture was, as Runciman says, the 'bloodthirsty proof of Christian fanaticism that re-created the fanaticism of Islam'.

The Summoning

'Hearken unto me, ye stouthearted,
that are far from righteousness.'
ISAIAH XLVI, 12

Pope Urban arrived in France in the late summer of 1095. On 5 August he was at Valence and on 11 August he reached Le Puy. From there he sent letters to the bishops of France and the neighbouring lands, requesting them to meet him at Clermont in November. Meanwhile he turned south, to spend September in Provence, at Avignon and Saint-Gilles. Early in October he was at Lyons and thence moved on into Burgundy. At Cluny, on 25 October, he consecrated the high altar of the great basilica that Abbot Hugh had begun to build. From Cluny he went to Souvigny, near Moulins, to pay his respects at the tomb of the holiest of Cluniac abbots, Saint Maiolus. There the Bishop of Clermont joined him, to escort him to his episcopal city, in readiness for the Council.

As he travelled Urban busied himself with the affairs of the Church in France, organizing and correcting, giving praise and blame where they were due. But his journeyings enabled him also to pursue his further scheme. We do not know whether, while he was in the south, he met in person Raymond of Saint-Gilles, Count of Toulouse and Marquis of Provence, already celebrated for his leadership of the holy wars in Spain. But he was in touch with him and must have heard of his experiences. At Cluny he could talk with men that were concerned with the pilgrim traffic, both to Compostella and to Jerusalem. They could tell him of the overwhelming difficulties that pilgrims to Palestine had now to endure with the disintegration of Turkish authority there. He learnt that not only were the roads across Asia Minor blocked, but the Holy Land itself was virtually closed to pilgrims.

The Council of Clermont sat from 18 November to 28 November 1095. Some three hundred clerics were present and their work covered a wide range. In general, decrees against lay investiture, simony and clerical marriage were repeated and the Truce of God was advocated. In particular, King Philip was excommunicated for adultery and the Bishop of Cambrai for simony, and the primacy of the see of Lyons over those of Sens and Reims was established. But the Pope wished to use the occasion for a more momentous purpose. It was announced that on Tuesday, 27 November, he would hold a public session, to make a great announcement. The crowds, clerical and lay, that assembled were too huge to be contained within the cathedral, where hitherto the Council had met. The Papal throne was set up on a platform in an open field outside the eastern gate of the city; and there, when the multitudes were gathered, Urban rose to his feet to address them.

Four contemporary chroniclers have reported the Pope's words for us. One of them, Robert the Monk, claims to have been present at the meeting. Baudri of Dol and Fulcher of Chartres write as though they had been present. The fourth, Guibert of Nogent, probably obtained his version at second hand. But none of them professes to give an accurate verbal account; and each wrote his chronicle a few years later and coloured his account in the light of subsequent events. We can only know approximately what Urban in fact said. It seems that he began his speech by telling his hearers of the necessity for aiding their brethren in the East. Eastern Christendom had appealed for help; for the Turks were advancing into the heart of Christian lands, maltreating the inhabitants and desecrating their shrines. But it was not only of Romania (which is Byzantium) that he spoke. He stressed the special holiness of Jerusalem and described the sufferings of the pilgrims that journeyed there. Having painted the sombre picture, he made his great appeal. Let western Christendom march to the rescue of the East. Rich and poor alike should go. They should leave off slaying each other and fight instead a righteous war, doing the work of God; and God would lead them. For those that died in battle there would be absolution and the remission of sins. Life was miserable and evil here, with men wearing themselves out to the ruin of their bodies and their souls. Here they were poor and unhappy; there they would be joyful and prosperous and true friends of God. There must be no delay. Let them be ready to set out when the summer had come, with God to be their guide.

Urban spoke with fervour and with all the art of a great orator. The response was immediate and tremendous. Cries of 'Deus le volt!' – 'God wills it!' – interrupted the speech. Scarcely had the Pope ended his words before the Bishop of Le Puy rose from his seat and, kneeling before the throne, begged permission to join in the holy expedition. Hundreds crowded up to follow his example. Then the Cardinal Gregory fell on his knees and loudly repeated the *Confiteor*; and all the vast audience echoed it after him. When the prayer was over Urban rose once more and pronounced the absolution and bade his hearers go home.

The enthusiasm was greater than Urban had expected. His plans for its direction were not yet fully made. No great lay lord had been present at Clermont. The recruits were all humbler men. It would be necessary to secure more solid secular support. In the meantime Urban reassembled his bishops for further consultation. The Council had probably already at his request passed a general decree giving remission from temporal penalties for the sins of all that took part with pious intentions in the holy war. It was now added that the worldly belongings of the participants should be placed under the protection of the Church during their absence at the war. The local bishop should be responsible for their safe-keeping and should return them intact when the warrior came home. Each member of the expedition was to wear the sign of the Cross, as a symbol of his dedication; a cross of red material should be sewn on to the shoulder of his surcoat. Anyone that took the Cross should vow to go to Jerusalem. If he turned back too soon or failed to set out, he would suffer excommunication. Clerics and monks were not to take the Cross without the permission of their bishop or abbot. The elderly and infirm must be discouraged from attempting the expedition; and no one at all should go without consulting his spiritual adviser. It was not to be a war of mere conquest. In all towns conquered from the infidel the churches of the East were to have all their rights and possessions restored to them. Everyone should be ready to leave his home by the Feast of the Assumption (15 August) next year, when the harvests should have been gathered; and the armies should assemble at Constantinople.

Next, a leader must be appointed. Urban wished to make it clear that the expedition was under the control of the Church. Its head must be an ecclesiastic, his legate. With the unanimous consent of the Council he nominated the Bishop of Le Puy.

Adhemar de Monteil, Bishop of Le Puy,

belonged to the family of the Counts of Valentinois. He was a middle-aged man, who had already made the pilgrimage to Jerusalem nine years before. He had earned his leadership by coming forward as the first to answer Urban's appeal; but as he had already entertained Urban at Le Puy in August and must have talked to him there of eastern affairs, it is possible that his stirring gesture was not entirely spontaneous. It was a wise appointment. Subsequent experience proved him to be a fine preacher and a tactful diplomat, broad-minded, calm and kindly, a man whom all would respect but who sought to persuade rather than to command. His influence was unfailingly used to curb passions and to spread goodwill, but it was not always firm enough to control the magnates that were nominally to be under his orders.

The first of the magnates to ask to join the expedition was Count Raymond of Toulouse. On 1 December, while Urban was still at Clermont, messengers arrived there to say that the Count and many of his nobility were eager to take the Cross. Raymond, who was at Toulouse, could not have heard reports of the great speech at Clermont. He must have had forewarning. As the first to be told of the project and the first to take the vow, he considered that he should be given the secular leadership over the other great lords. He wished to be Moses to Adhemar's Aaron. Urban would not admit this pretension; but Raymond never entirely abandoned it. In the meantime he planned to co-operate loyally with Adhemar.

Urban left Clermont on 2 December. After visiting various Cluniac houses he spent Christmas at Limoges, where he preached the Crusade in the cathedral, then passed northward through Poitiers to the valley of the Loire. In March he was at Tours, where he held a council; and one Sunday he summoned a congregation to meet him in a meadow by the banks of the river. Standing on an improvised platform he preached a long and solemn sermon, exhorting his hearers to repent and to go on the Crusade. From Tours he turned southward again through Aquitaine, past Saintes and Bordeaux to Toulouse. Toulouse was his head-quarters in May and June; and he had many opportunities for discussing the Crusade with his host, Count Raymond. Late in June he moved on to Provence. Raymond accompanied him to Nîmes.

In August the Pope recrossed the Alps into Lombardy. His journey had been no holiday. All the time he was interviewing churchmen and writing letters, seeking to complete his reorganization of the Church in France and, above all, continuing his plans for the Crusade. Synodal letters embodying the decisions taken at Clermont were sent round to the bishops of the West. In some cases provincial councils were held to receive them and to consider local action. It is probable that the chief lay powers were also officially informed of the Pope's desires. From Limoges at the end of 1095 Urban wrote to all the faithful in

Flanders referring them to the acts of the Council at Clermont and asking for their support. He had every reason to be satisfied with the response that came from Flanders and the neighbouring lands. In July 1096, while he was at Nimes, he received a message from King Philip announcing his absolute submission on the matter of his adultery and probably telling at the same time of the adhesion of his brother, Hugh of Vermandois, to the Crusade. During the same month Raymond of Toulouse gave proof of his intentions by handing over many of his possessions to the monastery of Saint-Gilles. It was perhaps on Raymond's advice that Urban decided that the help of a maritime power would be necessary in order to maintain the expedition's supplies. Two legates set out with letters to the republic of Genoa to ask for its co-operation. The republic agreed to provide twelve galleys and a transport, but cautiously delayed their dispatch till it could tell whether the Crusade was a serious movement. It was only in July 1097 that this fleet set sail from Genoa. Meanwhile many Genoese took the Cross.

By the time that Urban was back in Italy he was assured of the success of his scheme. His summons was eagerly obeyed. From as far afield as Scotland, Denmark and Spain, men hastened to make their vows. Some raised money for the journey by pawning their possessions and their lands. Others, expecting never to return, gave everything over to the Church. A sufficient number of great nobles had adhered to the Crusade to give it a formidable military backing. Beside Raymond of Toulouse and Hugh of Vermandois, Robert II of Flanders, Robert, Duke of Normandy, and the latter's brother-in-law Stephen, Count of Blois, were making preparations to set out. More remarkable was the adherence of men devoted to the emperor Henry IV. Chief amongst these was Godfrey of Bouillon, Duke of Lower Lorraine, who took the Cross with his brothers, Eustace, Count of Boulogne, and Baldwin. Grouped round these leaders were many of the lesser nobility and a few eminent ecclesiastics, such as the Bishop of Bayeux.

In Italy Urban found similar enthusiasm. In September 1096 he wrote to the city of Bologna to thank its citizens for their zeal and to caution them not to leave for the East without their priests' permission. Nor should newly married husbands leave without their wives' consent. Meanwhile news of the project had reached southern Italy and was warmly welcomed by many of the Normans there, who were always ready to start on a new adventure. The princes at first held back, but Guiscard's son Bohemond, now prince of Taranto but thwarted in his ambitions in Italy by his brother Roger Borsa and his uncle Roger of Sicily, soon realized the possibilities that the Crusade would open out for him. Together with many of his family and his friends, he took the Cross. Their participation brought to the movement many of the most experienced and enterprising soldiers in Europe. When Urban returned to Rome in time for Christmas 1096, he could feel assured that the Crusade was truly launched.

He had in fact launched a movement greater than he knew. It might have been better if fewer great lords had answered his appeal. For, though with all of them except Bohemond genuine religious fervour was the strongest motive, soon their terrestrial schemes and rivalries would create troubles far beyond the papal legate's control. Still more uncontrollable was the response shown by humbler folk throughout France and Flanders and the Rhineland.

The Pope had asked his bishops to preach the Crusade; but far more effective preaching was done by poorer men, by evangelicals such as Robert of Arbrissel, founder of the Order of Fontevrault, and still more by an itinerant monk called Peter. Peter was an oldish man, born somewhere near Amiens. He had probably tried to make the pilgrimage to Jerusalem a few years previously, but had been maltreated by the Turks and forced to turn back. His contemporaries knew him as Little Peter – *chtou* or *kiokio* in the Picard dialect – but later the hermit's cape that he habitually wore brought him the surname of 'the Hermit', by which he is better known to history. He was a man of short stature, swarthy and with a long, lean face, horribly like the donkey that he always rode and which was revered almost as much as himself. He went barefoot; and his clothes were filthy. He ate neither bread nor meat, but fish, and he drank wine. Despite his lowly appearance he had the power to move men. There was an air of strange authority about him. 'Whatever he said or did', Guibert of Nogent, who knew him personally, tells us, 'it seemed like something half-divine.'

Peter probably had not assisted at the Council of Clermont; but before the year 1095 was out he was already preaching the Crusade. He began his tour in Berry, then moved during February and March through Orléannais and Champagne into Lorraine, and thence past the cities of the Meuse and Aachen to Cologne, where he spent Easter. He gathered disciples whom he sent to the districts that he could not himself visit. Among them were the Frenchmen Walter Sans-Avoir, Rainald of Breis, Geoffrey Burel and Walter of Breteuil, and the Germans Orel and Gottschalk. Wherever he or his lieutenants went, men and women left their homes to follow him. By the time that he reached Cologne his train was estimated at about 15,000 persons; and many more joined him in Germany.

The extraordinary success of his preaching was due to many causes. Life for a peasant in north-western Europe was grim and insecure. Much land had gone out of cultivation during the barbarian invasions and the raids of the Norsemen. Dykes had been broken, and the sea and rivers had encroached on to the fields. The lords often opposed the clearing of the forests in which they hunted for their game. A village unprotected by a lord's castle was liable to be robbed or burnt by outlaws or by soldiers fighting petty civil wars. The Church sought to protect the poor peasants and to establish *bourgs* in empty lands; but its help was fitful and often unavailing. Greater lords might encourage the growth of towns, but lesser barons opposed it. The organiz-. ation of the demesne was breaking down, but no orderly system was taking its place. Though actual serfdom had vanished, men were tied to the land by obligations that they could not easily escape. Meanwhile the population was increasing, and holdings in a village could not be subdivided beyond a certain limit. 'In this land', said Urban at Clermont, according to Robert the Monk, 'you can scarcely feed the inhabitants. That is why you use up its goods and excite endless wars amongst yourselves.' Recent years had been especially diffi- cult. Floods and pestilence in 1094 had been followed by drought and a famine in 1095. It was a moment when emigration seemed very attrac- tive. Already in April 1095 a shower of meteorites had presaged a great movement of peoples.

Apocalyptic teaching added to the economic inducement. It was an age of visions; and Peter was thought to be a visionary. Medieval man was convinced that the Second Coming was at hand. He must repent while yet there was time and must go out to do good. The Church taught that sin could be expiated by pilgrimage and prophecies declared

that the Holy Land must be recovered for the faith
before Christ could come again. Further, to ignorant
minds the distinction between Jerusalem and the
New Jerusalem was not very clearly defined. Many
of Peter's hearers believed that he was promising
to lead them out of their present miseries to the
land flowing with milk and honey of which the
scriptures spoke. The journey would be hard; there
were the legions of Antichrist to be overcome. But
the goal was Jerusalem the golden.

What Pope Urban thought of Peter and the
success of his preaching no one now knows. His
letter to the Bolognese suggests that he was a little
nervous of uncontrolled enthusiasm; but he did
not, or could not, prevent it from spreading in
Italy. Throughout the summer of 1096 a casual but
constant stream of pilgrims without leaders or
any form of organization began to flow to the
East. No doubt he hoped that they and Peter's
followers would safely reach Constantinople and
there would await the coming of his legate and
the military chieftains, who would incorporate
them into the orderly ranks of the great Christian
army.

Urban's insistence that the expedition should
assemble at Constantinople shows how confident
he was that the Emperor Alexius would welcome
it. Byzantium had asked for soldiers from the West;
and here they were answering the summons, not
as a few individual mercenaries but in whole
powerful armies. His confidence was ingenuous.

No government is unwilling to make allies. But when these allies send large armies, over which it has no control, to invade its territory, expecting to be fed and housed and provided with every amenity, then it questions whether the alliance is worth while. When news of the Crusading movement reached Constantinople it aroused feelings of disquiet and alarm.

In 1096 the Byzantine Empire had been enjoying for some months a rare interval of repose. The Emperor had recently defeated a Cuman invasion of the Balkans so decisively that none of the barbarian tribes of the steppes was likely now to attempt to cross the frontier. In Asia Minor, thanks to civil wars encouraged by Byzantine diplomacy, the Seldjuk empire was beginning to disintegrate. Alexius hoped soon to take the offensive against it, but he wished to choose his own time. He still needed a breathing-space in which he could repair his strained resources. The problem of man-power worried him. He wished for mercenaries from the West; and no doubt he hoped that his ambassadors in Italy were successful in their recruitment. Now he was informed that instead of the individual knights or small companies that he expected to join his forces, whole Frankish armies were on the move. He was not pleased, as he knew from experience that the Franks were an unstable race, greedy for money and unscrupulous in keeping agreements. They were formidable in attack; but under the circumstances that was a doubtful advantage. It was with some apprehension that the imperial court learnt, in the words of the princess Anna Comnena, that 'all the West and all the barbarian tribes from beyond the Adriatic as far as the Pillars of Hercules were moving in a body through Europe towards Asia, bringing whole families with them'. Not only the Emperor but his subjects were uneasy. As a monitory portent great hordes of locusts swept over the Empire, leaving the corn untouched but devouring the vines. Inspired, perhaps, by a hint from the authorities who were anxious not to spread despondency, popular soothsayers interpreted this to mean that the Franks would do no harm to good Christians, whose symbol was the corn, the source of the bread of life, but would destroy the Saracens, a people whose sensuality might well be symbolized by the vine. The Princess Anna was a little sceptical of the interpretation; but the likeness of the Franks to locusts was certainly apparent.

The Emperor Alexius set about calmly making his preparations. The Frankish armies would have to be fed as they travelled through the Empire; and precautions must be taken to keep them from ravaging the countryside and robbing the inhabitants. Stores of provisions were accumulated in each main centre through which they would pass, and a police force was detailed to meet each detachment when it arrived within the Empire and to accompany it to Constantinople.

There were two great roads across the Balkan peninsula, the north road that crossed the frontier at Belgrade and struck south-east through Nish, Sofia, Philippopolis and Adrianople, and the Via Egnatia, from Dyrrhachium through Ochrida and Edessa (Vodena) to Thessalonica and on through Mosynopolis and Selymbria to the capital. Since the great German pilgrimage of 1064 the former road had seldom been used by travellers from the West. The total number of pilgrims had declined and those that had attempted the journey had preferred the alternative route. Moreover, Alexius received his information about the Crusade from Italy. He therefore anticipated that the Frankish armies would cross the Adriatic and make use of the Via Egnatia. Supplies were sent to Dyrrhachium and the intervening cities; and the governor of Dyrrhachium, the Emperor's nephew John Comnenus, was instructed to give the Frankish leaders a cordial welcome, but to see that they and their armies were all the time supervised by the military police. High-ranking envoys from Constantinople would be sent to greet each leader in turn. Meanwhile the admiral Nicholas Mavrocatacalon took a flotilla to Adriatic waters to watch the coasts and give warning of the approach of the Frankish transports.

The Emperor himself remained at Constantinople, awaiting further news. Knowing that the Pope had fixed 15 August as the date of departure for the expedition he did not hurry over his preparations, when suddenly, at the end of May 1096, a messenger came posting from the north to say that the first Frankish army had come down through Hungary and had entered the Empire at Belgrade.

The People's Crusade

'The Lord was not able to bring them into
the land which he promised them.'

DEUTERONOMY IX, 28

Peter the Hermit arrived with his followers at
Cologne on Holy Saturday, 12 April 1096. There he
began to realize the difficulties that beset the leader
of a popular expedition. The vast motley collection
of enthusiasts that he had gathered together
consisted of men from many districts and of many
types. Some brought their women with them,
some even their children. Most of them were peasants, but there were townsfolk among them, there
were junior members of knightly families, there were
former brigands and criminals. Their only link was
the fervour of their faith. All of them had given up
everything to follow Peter; and they were eager to
continue on their way. It was, moreover, essential
to keep them on the move if they were to be fed;
for few districts in medieval Europe had a sufficient
surplus of foodstuffs to supply for long the needs
of so large a company. But Cologne was set in a
rich countryside with good river communications.
Peter wished to take advantage of the facilities that

it provided to pause a while and preach to the Germans. He was probably anxious to attract some of the local nobility to his Crusade. In France and Flanders the knights preferred to join the company of some great lord. But no great German lord was going to the holy war. His preaching was successful. Among the many Germans that answered his call were several of the lesser nobility, led by Count Hugh of Tübingen, Count Henry of Schwarzenberg, Walter of Teck and the three sons of the Count of Zimmern.

But the Frenchmen were impatient. Walter Sans-Avoir decided that he would not wait at Cologne. With a few thousand compatriots he left the city as soon as the Easter Feast was over, probably on Easter Tuesday, and set out on the road to Hungary. Marching up the Rhine and the Neckar and down the Danube, he reached the Hungarian frontier on 8 May. There he sent to King Coloman to ask for permission to cross the kingdom and for help in obtaining provisions for his men. Coloman proved friendly. The army passed through Hungary without an untoward incident. About the end of the month it reached Semlin on the further frontier, and crossed the Rive Save into Byzantine territory at Belgrade.

The military commander at Belgrade was taken by surprise. He had received no instructions how to deal with such an invasion. He sent post-haste to Nish, where the governor of the Bulgarian province resided, to inform him of Walter's arrival. The governor, a conscientious but undistinguished offi-

cial called Nicetas, was equally uninstructed. In his
turn he dispatched a messenger to take the news as
quickly as possible to Constantinople. Meanwhile
Walter at Belgrade demanded food for his
followers. The harvests were not yet gathered, and
the garrison had none to spare; so Walter and his
troops began to pillage the countryside. His
temper was inflamed owing to an unfortunate
occurrence at Semlin, where sixteen of his men,
who had not crossed the river with their compan-
ions, tried to rob a bazaar. The Hungarians
captured them and stripped them of their arms
and their clothing, which were hung on the walls
of Semlin as a warning, and sent them on naked
across to Belgrade. When the pillaging round
Belgrade began the commander resorted to arms.
In the fighting several of Walter's men were killed
and others were burnt alive in a church.

Walter was eventually able to march on to Nish,
where Nicetas received him kindly and provided
food, keeping him there till he received an answer
from Constantinople. The Emperor, who had
believed that the Crusade would not leave the West
before the Feast of the Assumption, was forced to
speed up his arrangements. Nicetas was requested
to send Walter on under escort. Accompanied by
this escort Walter and his army continued their
journey in peace. Early in July they reached
Philippopolis, where Walter's uncle, Walter of
Poissy, died; and by the middle of the month they
were in Constantinople.

From Walter Nicetas must have learnt that Peter was not far behind, with a far larger company. He therefore moved up to Belgrade to meet him and made contact with the Hungarian governor of Semlin.

Peter left Cologne on about 20 April. The Germans at first had mocked at his preaching; but by now many thousands had joined him, till his followers probably numbered close on 20,000 men and women. Other Germans, fired by his enthusiasm, planned to follow later, under Gottschalk and Count Emich of Leisingen. From Cologne Peter took the usual road up the Rhine and the Neckar to the Danube. When they reached the Danube, some of his company decided to travel by boat down the river; but Peter and his main body marched by the road running south of Lake Ferto and entered Hungary at Oedenburg. Peter himself rode on his donkey, and the German knights on horseback, while lumbering wagons carried such stores as he possessed and the chest of money that he had collected for the journey. But the vast majority travelled on foot. Where the roads were good they managed to cover twenty-five miles a day.

King Coloman received Peter's emissaries with the same benevolence that he had shown to Walter, warning them only that any attempt to pillage would be punished. The army moved peaceably through Hungary during late May and early June. At some point, probably near Karlovci, it was rejoined by the detachments that had travelled by boat. On 20 June it reached Semlin.

There its troubles began. What actually happened is obscure. It seems that the governor, who was a Ghuzz Turk in origin, was alarmed by the size of the army. Together with his colleague across the frontier he attempted to tighten up police regulations. Peter's army was suspicious. It heard rumours of the sufferings of Walter's men; it feared that the two governors were plotting against it; and it was shocked by the sight of the arms of Walter's sixteen miscreants still hanging on the city walls. But all might have been well had not a dispute arisen over the sale of a pair of shoes. This led to a riot, which turned into a pitched battle. Probably against Peter's wishes, his men, led by Geoffrey Burel, attacked the town and succeeded in storming the citadel. Four thousand Hungarians were killed and a large store of provisions captured. Then, terrified of the vengeance of the Hungarian king, they made all haste to cross the river Save.

They took all the wood that they could collect from the houses, with which to build themselves rafts. Nicetas, watching anxiously from Belgrade, tried to control the crossing of the river, and to oblige them to use one ford only. His troops were mainly composed of Petcheneg mercenaries, men that could be trusted to obey his orders blindly. They were sent in barges to prevent any crossing except at the proper place. He himself, recognizing that he had insufficient troops for dealing with such a horde, retired back to Nish, where the military headquarters of the province were placed. On his departure the inhabitants of Belgrade deserted the town and took to the mountains.

On 26 June Peter's army forced its way across the Save. When the Petchenegs tried to restrict them to one passage, they were attacked. Several of the boats were sunk and the soldiers aboard captured and put to death. The army entered Belgrade and set fire to it, after a wholesale pillage. Then it marched on for seven days through the forests and arrived at Nish on 3 July, Peter sent at once to Nicetas to ask for supplies of food.

Nicetas had informed Constantinople of Peter's approach, and was awaiting the officials and military escort that were coming to convoy the westerners on to the capital. He had a large garrison at Nish; and he had strengthened it by recruiting locally additional Petcheneg and Hungarian mercenaries. But he probably could not spare any men to act as Peter's escort until the troops from Constantinople should meet him. On the other hand it was impracticable and dangerous to allow so vast a company to linger long at Nish. Peter was requested therefore to provide hostages while food was collected for his men and then to move on as soon as possible. All went well at first. Geoffrey Burel and Walter of Breteuil were handed over as hostages. The local inhabitants not only allowed the Crusaders to acquire the supplies that they needed, but many of them gave alms to the poorer pilgrims. Some even asked to join the pilgrimage.

Next morning the Crusaders started out along the road to Sofia. As they were leaving the town some Germans who had quarrelled with a townsman on the previous night wantonly set fire to a group of mills by the river. Hearing of this, Nicetas sent troops to attack the rearguard and to take some prisoners whom he could hold as hostages. Peter was riding his donkey about a mile ahead and knew nothing of all this till a man called Lambert ran up from the rear to tell him. He hurried back to interview Nicetas and to arrange for the ransom of the captives. But while they were conferring, rumours of fighting and of treachery spread round the army. A company of hotheads thereupon turned and assailed the fortifications of the town. The garrison drove them off and counter-attacked; then while Peter, who had gone to restrain his men, tried to re-establish contact with Nicetas, another group insisted upon renewing the attack. Nicetas therefore let all his forces loose on the Crusaders, who were completely routed and scattered. Many of them were slain; many were captured, men, women and children, and spent the rest of their days in captivity in the neighbourhood. Amongst other things Peter lost his money-chest. Peter himself, with Rainald of Breis and Walter of Breteuil and about five hundred men, fled up a mountain-side, believing that they alone survived. But next morning seven thousand others caught them up; and they continued on the road. At the deserted town of Bela Palanka they paused to gather the local harvest, as they had no food left. There many more stragglers joined them. When they continued on their march they found that a quarter of their company had been lost.

They reached Sofia on 12 July. There they met the envoys and the escort, sent from Constantinople with orders to keep them fully supplied and to see that they never delayed anywhere for more than three days. Thenceforward their journey passed smoothly. The local population was friendly. At Philippopolis the Greeks were so deeply moved by the stories of their suffering that they freely gave them money, horses and mules. Two days outside Adrianople more envoys greeted Peter with a gracious message from the Emperor. It was decided that the expedition should be forgiven for its crimes, as it had been already sufficiently punished. Peter wept with joy at the favour shown him by so great a potentate.

The Emperor's kindly interest did not cease when the Crusaders arrived at Constantinople on 1 August. He was curious to see its leader; and Peter was summoned to an audience at the court, where he was given money and good advice. To Alexius's experienced eye the expedition was not impressive. He feared that if it crossed into Asia it would soon be destroyed by the Turks. But its indiscipline obliged him to move it as soon as possible from the neighbourhood of Constantinople. The westerners committed endless thefts. They broke into the palaces and villas in the suburbs; they even stole the lead from the roofs of churches. Though their entry into Constantinople itself was strictly controlled, only small parties of sightseers being admitted through the gates, it was impossible to police the whole neighbourhood.

Walter Sans-Avoir and his men were already at Constantinople, and various bands of Italian pilgrims arrived there about the same time. They joined up with Peter's expedition; and on 6 August the whole of his forces were conveyed across the Bosphorus. From the Asiatic shore they marched in an unruly manner, pillaging houses and churches, along the coast of the Sea of Marmora to Nicomedia, which lay deserted since its sack by the Turks fifteen years before. There a quarrel broke out between the Germans and the Italians on the one side and the French on the other. The former broke away from Peter's command and elected as their leader an Italian lord called Rainald. At Nicomedia the two parts of the army turned westward along the south coast of the Gulf of Nicomedia to a fortified camp called Cibotos by the Greeks and Civetot by the Crusaders, which Alexius had prepared for the use of his own English mercenaries in the neighbourhood of Helenopolis. It was a convenient camping-ground, as the district was fertile and further supplies could easily be brought by sea from Constantinople.

Alexius had urged Peter to await the coming of the main Crusading armies before attempting any attack on the infidel; and Peter was impressed by his advice. But Peter's authority was waning. Both the Germans and Italians, under Rainald, and his own Frenchmen, over whom Geoffrey Burel seems to have held the chief influence, instead of quietly recuperating their strength, vied with each other in raiding the countryside. First they pillaged the immediate neighbourhood; then they cautiously advanced into territory held by the Turks, making forays and robbing the villagers, who were all Christian Greeks. In the middle of September several thousand of the Frenchmen ventured as far as the gates of Nicaea, the capital of the Seldjuk Sultan, Kilij Arslan ibn-Suleiman. They sacked the villages in the suburbs, rounding up the flocks and herds that they found and torturing and massacring the Christian inhabitants with horrifying savagery. It was said that they roasted babies on spits. A Turkish detachment sent out from the city was driven off after a fierce combat. They then returned to Civetot, where they sold their booty to their comrades and to the Greek sailors who were about the camp.

This profitable French raid roused the jealousy of the Germans. Towards the end of September Rainald set out with a German expedition of some six thousand men, including priests and even bishops. They marched beyond Nicaea, pillaging as they went, but, kinder than the Frenchmen, sparing the Christians, till they came to a castle called Xerigordon. This they managed to capture; and, finding it well stocked with provisions of every sort, they planned to make it a centre from which they could raid the countryside. On hearing of the Crusaders' exploit, the Sultan sent a high military commander with a large force to recapture the castle. Xerigordon was set on a hill, and its water supply came from a well just outside the walls and a spring in the valley below. The Turkish army, arriving before the castle on St Michael's Day, 29 September, defeated an ambush laid by Rainald and, taking possession of the spring and the well, kept the Germans closely invested within the castle. Soon the besieged grew desperate from thirst. They tried to suck moisture from the earth; they cut the veins of their horses and donkeys to drink their blood; they even drank each other's urine. Their priests tried vainly to comfort and encourage them. After eight days of agony Rainald decided to surrender. He opened the gates to the enemy on receiving a promise that his life would be spared if he renounced Christianity. Everyone that remained true to the faith was slaughtered. Rainald and those that apostasized with him were sent into captivity, to Antioch and to Aleppo and far into Khorassan.

News of the capture of Xerigordon by the Germans had reached the camp at Civetot early in October. It was followed by a rumour, spread by two Turkish spies, that they had taken Nicaea itself and were dividing up the booty for their benefit. As the Turks expected, this caused tumultuous excitement in the camp. The soldiers clamoured to be allowed to hasten to Nicaea, along roads that the Sultan had carefully ambushed. Their leaders had difficulty in restraining them, till suddenly the truth was discovered about the fate of Rainald's expedition. The excitement was changed to panic; and the chiefs of the army met to discuss what next to do. Peter had gone to Constantinople. His authority over the army had vanished. He hoped to revive it by obtaining some important material aid from the Emperor. There was a movement in the army to go out to avenge Xerigordon. But Walter Sans-Avoir persuaded his colleagues to await Peter's return, which was due in eight days' time. Peter, however, did not return; and meanwhile it was reported that the Turks were approaching in force towards Civetot. The army council met again. The more responsible leaders, Walter Sans-Avoir, Rainald of Breis, Walter of Breteuil and Fulk of Orleans, and the Germans, Hugh of Tübingen and Walter of Teck, still urged that nothing should be done till Peter arrived. But Geoffrey Burel, with the public opinion of the army behind him, insisted that it would be cowardly and foolish not to advance against the enemy. He had his way. On 21 October, at dawn, the whole army of the Crusaders, numbering over 20,000 men, marched out from Civetot, leaving behind them only old men, women and children and the sick.

Barely three miles from the camp, where the road to Nicaea entered a narrow wooded valley, by a village called Dracon, the Turks were lying in ambush. The Crusaders marched noisily and carelessly, the knights on horseback at their head. Suddenly a hail of arrows from the woods killed or maimed the horses; and as they plunged in confusion, unseating their riders, the Turks attacked. The cavalry, pursued by the Turks, was flung back on to the infantry. Many of the knights fought bravely, but they could not stop the panic that seized the army. In a few minutes the whole host was fleeing in utter disorder to Civetot. There in the camp the daily round was just beginning. Some of the older folk were still asleep in their beds. Here and there a priest was celebrating early mass. Into its midst there burst a horde of terrified fugitives with the enemy on their heels. There was no real resistance. Soldiers, women and priests were massacred before they had time to move. Some fled into the forests around, others into the sea, but few of them escaped for long. Others defended themselves for a while by lighting bonfires which the wind blew into the Turks' faces. Only young boys and girls whose appearance pleased the Turks were spared, together with a few captives made after the first heat of the fighting was over. These were taken away into slavery. Some three thousand, luckier than the rest, managed to reach an old castle that stood by the sea. It had long been out of use, and its doors and windows were dismantled. But the refugees, with the energy of despair, improvised fortifications from the wood that lay about and reinforced them with bones, and were able to beat off the attacks of the enemy.

The castle held out; but elsewhere on the field by midday all was over. Corpses covered the ground from the pass of Dracon to the sea. Amongst the dead were Walter Sans-Avoir, Rainald of Breis, Fulk of Orleans, Hugh of Tübingen, Walter of Teck, Conrad and Albert of Zimmern and many other of the German knights. The only leaders to survive were Geoffrey Burel, whose impetuousness had caused the disaster, Walter of Breteuil and William of Poissy, Henry of Schwarzenberg, Frederick of Zimmern and Rudolf of Brandis, almost all of whom were badly wounded.

When dusk fell a Greek who was with the army succeeded in finding a boat and set sail for Constantinople, to tell Peter and the Emperor of the battle. Of Peter's feelings we have no record; but Alexius at once ordered some men-of-war, with strong forces aboard, to sail for Civetot. On the arrival of the Byzantine battle-squadron the Turks raised the siege of the castle and retired inland. The survivors were taken off to the ships and returned to Constantinople. There they were given quarters in the suburbs; but their arms were removed from them.

The People's Crusade was over. It had cost

many thousands of lives; it had tried the patience of the Emperor and his subjects; and it had taught that faith alone, without wisdom and discipline, would not open the road to Jerusalem.

The Capture of Nicaea

'And thou shalt come from thy place out of the north
parts, thou, and many people with thee, all of them riding
upon horses, a great company, and a mighty army.'

EZEKIEL XXXVIII, 15

However much the Emperor and the Crusader
princes might quarrel over their ultimate rights and
the distribution of conquests to come, there could
be no dissension about the opening stages of the
campaign against the infidel. If the Crusade was to
reach Jerusalem, the roads across Asia Minor must
be cleared; and to drive the Turk out of Asia Minor
was the chief aim of Byzantine policy. There was
complete agreement on strategy; and as yet, with
a Byzantine army by their side, the Crusaders were
willing to defer to its experienced generals on
matters of tactics.

The first objective was the Seldjuk capital,
Nicaea. Nicaea lay on the shores of the Ascanian
lake, not far from the Sea of Marmora. The old
Byzantine military road ran through it, though
there was an alternative route passing a little
further to the east. To leave this great fortress in
enemy hands would endanger all communications

across the country. Alexius was eager to move the Crusaders on as soon as possible, as summer was advancing; and the Crusaders themselves were impatient. In the last days of April, before the northern French army had arrived at Constantinople, orders were given to prepare to strike the camp at Pelecanum and to advance on Nicaea.

The moment was well chosen; for the Seldjuk Sultan, Kilij Arslan I, was away on his eastern frontier, contesting with the Danishmend princes for the suzerainty of Melitene, whose Armenian ruler, Gabriel, was busily embroiling the neighbouring potentates with each other. Kilij Arslan did not take seriously this new menace from the West. His easy defeat of Peter the Hermit's rabble taught him to despise the Crusaders; and perhaps his spies in Constantinople, wishing to please their master, gave him exaggerated accounts of the quarrels between the Emperor and the western princes. Believing that the Crusade would never penetrate to Nicaea, he left his wife and children and all his treasure inside its walls. It was only when he received news of the enemy concentration at Pelecanum that he sent part of his army hurrying back westward, following himself as soon as he could arrange his affairs in the east. His troops arrived too late to interfere with the Crusaders' march on Nicaea.

Godfrey of Lorraine's army left Pelecanum on about 26 April, and marched to Nicomedia, where it waited for three days and was joined by Bohemond's army, under the command of Tancred, and by Peter the Hermit and the remains of his rabble. Bohemond himself stayed on for a few days at Constantinople, to arrange with the Emperor for the provision of supplies to the army. A small Byzantine detachment of engineers with siege engines accompanied the troops, under the leadership of Manuel Butumites. From Nicomedia Godfrey led the army to Civetot, then turned south through the defile where Peter's men had perished. Their bones still covered the entrance to the pass; and, warned by their fate and by the advice of the Emperor, Godfrey moved cautiously, sending scouts and engineers in front, to clear and widen the track; which was then marked by a series of wooden crosses, to serve as a guide for future pilgrims. On 6 May he arrived before Nicaea. The city had been strongly fortified since the fourth century; and its walls, some four miles in length, with their two hundred and forty towers, had been kept in constant repair by the Byzantines. It lay on the eastern end of the Ascanian Lake, its west walls rising straight out of the shallow water, and it formed an uneven pentagon. Godfrey encamped outside the northern wall and Tancred outside the eastern wall. The southern wall was left for Raymond's army.

The Turkish garrison was large but needed reinforcements. Messengers, one of whom was intercepted by the Crusaders, were sent to the

Sultan to urge him to rush troops into the city through the south gates, before its investment was complete. But the Turkish army was still too far away. Before its vanguard could approach, Raymond arrived, on 16 May, and spread his army before the southern wall. Bohemond had joined his army two or three days sooner. Till he came, insufficient provisions had weakened the Crusaders; but, thanks to his arrangements with Alexius, henceforward supplies flowed freely to the besiegers, coming both by land and by sea. When Robert of Normandy and Stephen of Blois arrived with their forces on 3 June, the whole Crusading army was assembled. It worked together as a single unit, though there was no one supreme commander. Decisions were taken by the princes acting in council. As yet there was no serious discord between them. Meanwhile the Emperor moved out to Pelecanum, where he could keep in touch both with his capital and with Nicaea.

The first Turkish relieving force reached Nicaea immediately after Raymond, to find the city entirely blockaded by land. After a brief, unsuccessful skirmish with Raymond's troops it withdrew, to await the main Turkish army which was approaching under the leadership of the Sultan. Alexius had instructed Butumites to establish contact with the besieged garrison. When it saw its relief retreating, its leaders invited Butumites under a safe-conduct into the town, to discuss terms of surrender. He accepted; but almost at once news came that the Sultan was not far away; and negotiations were broken off.

It was on about 21 May that the Sultan and his army came up from the south and at once attacked the Crusaders in an attempt to force an entrance into the city. Raymond, with the Bishop of Le Puy in command of his right flank, bore the brunt of the attack; for neither Godfrey nor Bohemond could venture to leave his section of the walls unguarded. But Robert of Flanders and his troops came to Raymond's aid. The battle raged fiercely all day; but the Turks could make no headway. When night fell the Sultan decided to retreat. The Crusader army was stronger than he had thought; and, man for man, his Turks were no match for the well-armed westerners in the open ground in front of the city. It was better strategy to retreat into the mountains and to leave the city to its fate.

The Crusaders' losses had been heavy. Many had been killed, including Baldwin, Count of Ghent; and almost all the surviving participants in the battle had been wounded. But the victory filled them with elation. To their delight they found among the Turkish dead the ropes brought to bind the prisoners that the Sultan had hoped to take. To weaken the morale of the besieged garrison they cut off the heads of many of the enemy corpses and threw them over the walls or fixed them on pikes to parade them before the gates. Then, with no more danger to fear from outside, they concentrated on the siege. But the fortifications were formidable. In vain Raymond and Adhemar attempted to mine one of the southern towers by sending sappers to dig beneath it and there to light a huge fire. The little damage that was done was repaired during the night by the garrison. Moreover it was found that the blockade was incomplete; for supplies still reached the city from across the lake. The Crusaders were obliged to ask the Emperor to come to their help and to provide boats to intercept this water route. Alexius was probably well aware of the position but wished the western princes to discover how necessary his co-operation was to them. At their request he provided a small flotilla for the lake, under the command of Butumites.

The Sultan, when he retired, had told the garrison to do as it thought best, as he could give no more aid. When it saw the Byzantine ships on the lake and understood that the Emperor was fully assisting the Crusaders it decided upon surrender. This was what Alexius had hoped. He had no wish to add a half-destroyed city to his dominions nor that his future subjects should undergo the horrors of a sack, especially as the majority of the citizens were Christians; for the Turks comprised only the soldiers and a small court nobility. Contact was re-established with Butumites, and the terms of surrender were discussed. But the Turks still hesitated, hoping, perhaps, that the Sultan would return. It was only on the news that the Crusaders were planning a general assault that at last they gave in.

The assault was ordered for 19 June. But when morning broke the Crusaders saw the Emperor's standard waving over the city towers. The Turks had surrendered during the night; and imperial troops, mainly Petcheneg, had entered the city through the gates on the lakeside. It is unlikely that the Crusading leaders had not been informed of the negotiations; nor did they disapprove, for they saw that it was pointless to waste time and men on storming a town that would not be theirs to hold. But they were deliberately kept in ignorance of the final stages; while the rank and file considered themselves cheated of their prey. They had hoped to pillage the riches of Nicaea. Instead, they were only allowed in small groups into the city, closely surveyed by the Emperor's police.

The Assault on Jerusalem

'Shout unto God with the voice of triumph.
For the Lord most high is terrible.'

PSALMS XLVII, 1, 2

The city of Jerusalem was one of the great fortresses of the medieval world. Since the days of the Jebusites its site had been famed for its strength, which the skill of men had improved down the centuries. The walls beneath which the Crusaders found themselves followed the same line as the walls built later by the Ottoman Sultan, Suleiman the Magnificent, which surround the old city to-day. They had been laid out when Hadrian rebuilt the city; and the Byzantines, the Ommayads and the Fatimids in turn had added to them and repaired them. On the east the wall was protected by the steep slopes of the ravine of the Kedron. On the south-east the ground fell to the Vale of Gehenna. A third valley that was only slightly less deep skirted the western wall. It was only on the south-west, where the wall cut across Mount Sion, and along the length of the northern wall that the terrain favoured an attack on the fortifications. The citadel, the Tower of David, was placed halfway down the western wall, commanding the road that slanted up the hill-side to the Jaffa Gate. Though there were no springs within the city, its ample cisterns secured the water supply. The Roman drainage system, still in use in the twentieth century, kept it from disease.

The defence of the city was in the hands of the Fatimid governor, Iftikhar ad-Dawla. The walls were in good condition; and he had a strong garrison of Arab and Sudanese troops. On the news of the Franks' approach he took the precaution of blocking or poisoning the wells outside the city, and driving the flocks and herds from the pastures round the city into places of safety. Next, he ordered all the Christian population of the city, Orthodox and heretic alike, to retire outside the city walls. The Jews, however, were permitted to remain within. It was a wise move. In the tenth century the Christians outnumbered the Moslems in Jerusalem; and though the Caliph Hakim's persecutions had reduced their numbers, and though many more, including most of the Orthodox clergy, had departed with the Patriarch during the uneasy times that followed Ortoq's death, there were still thousands left, useless as fighting men as they were forbidden to carry arms, and unreliable in a battle against fellow-Christians. Moreover their exile meant that there would be fewer mouths to feed in the beleaguered city. At the same time Iftikhar sent urgently to Egypt for armed aid.

Even had the lie of the land permitted it, the Crusaders had insufficient forces to invest the whole city. They concentrated their strength on the sectors where they could come near to the walls. Robert of Normandy took up his station along the northern wall opposite to the Gate of Flowers (Herod's Gate), with Robert of Flanders on his right, opposite to the Gate of the Column (St Stephen's or the Damascus Gate). Godfrey of Lorraine took over the area covering the north-west angle of the city, as far down as the Jaffa Gate. He was joined here by Tancred, who rode up when the army was already in position, bringing flocks that he had taken on his way from Bethlehem. To his south was Raymond of Toulouse, who, finding that the valley kept him too far from the walls, moved up after two or three days on to Mount Sion. The eastern and south-eastern sectors were left unguarded.

The siege began on 7 June, the very day that the Crusade arrived at the walls. But it was soon clear that time was on the side of the besieged. Iftikhar was well supplied with food and water. His armaments were better than the Franks'; and he was able to strengthen his towers with sacks full of cotton and of hay, which enabled them to withstand the shock of the bombardment by the Frankish mangonels. If he could hold out till the relieving army from Egypt appeared, all would be over with the Crusade. But, large though the garrison was, it was barely sufficient to man all the walls. The Crusaders on their part soon were in difficulties over their water supply. Iftikhar's measures had been effective. The only source of pure water available to the besiegers came from the pool of Siloam, below the south walls, which was dangerously exposed to missiles from the city. To supplement their supplies of water, they had to travel six miles or more. Knowing this, the garrison would send out small companies to ambush the paths to the springs. Many soldiers and pilgrims perished from such surprise attacks. Food also began to run short; for little could be obtained near the city. Heat and dust and lack of shade added to the discomfort of the Crusaders, coming as they did from cooler climates and wearing, many of them, armour ill-suited to the Judaean summer. It was clear to them all that they could not afford a long siege but must quickly take the city by assault.

On 12 June the princes made a pilgrimage to the Mount of Olives. There an aged hermit addressed them, bidding them attack the walls on the morrow. They protested that they lacked the machines for a successful assault; but the hermit would have none of that. If they had faith, God, he said, would give them the victory. Emboldened by his words, they ordered a general attack to be made next morning. But the hermit was mistaken or else their faith was too weak. The Crusaders went to the attack with great fervour and soon overran the outer defences of the north wall. But they had too few ladders to be able to scale the walls simultaneously in a sufficient number of places. After several hours of desperate fighting they saw that their attempts were useless and withdrew.

The failure of the assault caused bitter disappointment; but it made clear to the princes the need for building more siege machines. At a council on 15 June they decided to withhold further attacks till they were better supplied with mangonels and ladders. But they lacked the material with which to build them. As at Antioch, they were now saved by the timely arrival of help from the sea. On 17 June six Christian vessels put into the harbour of Jaffa, which they found deserted by the Moslems. The squadron consisted of two Genoese galleys, under the brothers Embriaco, and four ships probably from the English fleet. They were carrying food supplies and armaments, including the ropes, nails and bolts required for making siege machines. Hearing of their arrival the Crusaders at once sent a small detachment to establish contact with them. Near Ramleh these troops were ambushed by a Moslem company, operating from Ascalon, and were only rescued by the coming of Raymond Pilet and his men close on their heels. Meanwhile an Egyptian fleet appeared off the coast and blockaded Jaffa. One of the English ships slipped through the blockade and sailed back to Lattakieh. The other ships were abandoned by their crews as soon as the cargo was landed; and the sailors marched up under Raymond Pilet's escort to the camp outside Jerusalem. They themselves and the goods that they brought were very welcome. But it was still necessary to find wood with which to build the machines. Little was to be obtained on the bare hills round Jerusalem; and the Crusaders were obliged to send expeditions for many miles to collect what was required. It was only when Tancred and Robert of Flanders penetrated with their followers as far as the forests round Samaria and came back laden with logs and planks carried on camel-back or by captive Moslems, that work could start upon the machines. Scaling-ladders were made; and Raymond and Godfrey each began to construct a wooden castle fitted with catapults and set on wheels. Gaston of Béarn was responsible for the construction of Godfrey's castle, and William Ricou of Raymond's.

But the work went slowly; and meanwhile the Franks suffered terribly from the heat. For many days the sirocco blew, with its deadly effect on the nerves of men unused to it. The provision of water grew increasingly difficult. Numbers of the pack-animals and the herds that the army had collected died daily from thirst. Detachments would go as far as the Jordan to find water. The native Christians were well-disposed and acted as guides to the springs and the forests of the neighbour-hood; but it was impossible to prevent forays and ambushes from Moslem soldiers, either of the garrison or of companies that were wandering freely round the country. Quarrels arose again among the princes, concerning, first, the possession of Bethlehem. Tancred had liberated the town and had left his banner waving over the Church of the Nativity. But the clergy and the rival princes felt it to be wrong that so holy a building should be in the power of one secular lord. Tancred defended his claims to Bethlehem; and, though public opinion was against him, the matter was deferred. Next, discussions were begun about the future status of Jerusalem. Some of the knights suggested that a king should be appointed; but the clergy unanimously opposed this, saying that no Christian could call himself king in the city where Christ was crowned and suffered. Here again public opinion was on the side of the clergy; and further discussions were postponed. Their physical miseries, combined with disappointment at the failure of the attempted assault and the renewed quarrels of the princes, induced many of the Crusaders even now to desert the Crusade. A company of them went down to the Jordan to undergo rebaptism in the holy river; then, after gathering palm branches from the river bank, they journeyed straight down to Jaffa, hoping to find boats to carry them back to Europe.

Early in July it was learnt in the camp that a great army had set out from Egypt to relieve

Jerusalem. The princes realized that there was no time for delay. But the morale of their men was low. Once more a vision came to their support. On the morning of 6 July the priest Peter Desiderius, who had already testified that he had seen Bishop Adhemar* after his death, came to Adhemar's brother, William Hugh of Monteil and to his own lord, Isoard of Gap, to say that the bishop had again appeared to him. After ordering the Crusaders to give up their selfish schemes, Adhemar ordered them to hold a fast and to walk in procession barefoot round the walls of Jerusalem. If they did so with repentant hearts, within nine days they would capture Jerusalem. When Peter Desiderius had claimed to see Adhemar suffering hell-fire for his doubting of the Holy Lance, he had been widely disbelieved; but now, perhaps because the beloved bishop was shown in a nobler light, and because the family of Monteil gave their support, the vision was at once accepted as genuine by all the army. Adhemar's instructions were eagerly obeyed. A fast was commanded and steadfastly observed during the next three days. On Friday, 8 July, a solemn procession wound around the path that surrounded the city. The bishops and priests of the Crusade came first, bearing crosses and their holy relics. The princes and the knights followed, then the foot soldiers and the pilgrims.

* The crusade's spiritual leader, Adhemar, had died in Antioch.

All were barefoot. The Moslems gathered on the walls to mock them; but they gloried in such mockery, and having completed the circuit ascended the Mount of Olives. There Peter the Hermit preached to them and after him Raymond's chaplain, Raymond of Aguilers, and Robert of Normandy's chaplain, Arnulf of Rohes, who was now considered the finest preacher with the army. Their eloquence moved and excited the host. Even Raymond and Tancred forgot their quarrels and vowed to fight together for the Cross.

The enthusiasm lasted on. During the next two days, in spite of their sufferings from thirst, the men of the army worked hard to complete the great siege towers. The skill of the Genoese, under William Embriaco, was of great assistance; and even the old men and the women did their part in sewing ox-hide and camel-hide and nailing it on the exposed parts of the woodwork, as a protection against the Greek fire used by the Saracens. On the 10th the wooden structures were ready and were wheeled up to their stations, the one against the north wall and the other on Mount Sion. A third, slightly smaller, was built to go against the north-west corner of the defences. The work of construction had been carefully carried on out of sight of the soldiers of the garrison; who were astounded and alarmed to find such castles opposing them. The governor, Iftikhar, hastened to reinforce the weaker sections of the defences; and the siege towers were steadily bombarded with stones and with liquid fire to prevent them from closing in against the walls.

It was decided that the assault should begin during the night of 13–14 July. The main attack would be launched simultaneously from Mount Sion and on the eastern sector of the northern wall, with a feint attack on the north-west angle. According to Raymond of Aguilers, whose figures need not be doubted, the effective fighting strength of the army was now twelve thousand foot-soldiers and twelve or thirteen hundred knights. There were in addition many pilgrims, whose numbers he does not try to assess, men too old or too sick to fight, and women and children. The first task of the assailants was to bring their wooden castles right up to the walls; which involved the filling up of the ditch that ran round their feet. All night long and during the day of the 14th the Crusaders concentrated on their task, suffering heavily from the stones and the liquid fire of the defence, and answering with a heavy bombardment from their own mangonels. By the evening of the 14th Raymond's men had succeeded in wheeling their tower over the ditch against the wall. But the defence was fierce; for it seems that Iftikhar himself commanded in this sector. Raymond could not establish a foothold on the wall itself. Next morning Godfrey's tower closed in on the north wall, close to the present Gate of Flowers.

Godfrey and his brother, Eustace of Boulogne, commanded from the upper storey. About midday they succeeded in making a bridge from the tower to the top of the wall; and two Flemish knights, Litold and Gilbert of Tournai, led the pick of the Lotharingian army across, followed soon by Godfrey himself. Once a sector of the wall was captured, scaling ladders enabled many more of the assailants to climb into the city. While Godfrey remained on the wall encouraging the newcomers and sending men to open the Gate of the Column to the main forces of the Crusade, Tancred and his men, who had been close behind the Lorrainers, penetrated deep into the city streets. The Moslems, seeing their defences broken, fled towards the Haram es-Sherif, the Temple area, where the Dome of the Rock and the Mosque of al-Aqsa stood, intending to use the latter as their last fortress. But they had no time to put it into a state of defence. As they crowded in and up on the roof, Tancred was upon them. Hastily they surrendered to him, promising a heavy ransom, and took his banner to display it over the mosque. He had already desecrated and pillaged the Dome of the Rock. Meanwhile the inhabitants of the city fled back in confusion towards the southern quarters, where Iftikhar was still holding out against Raymond. Early in the afternoon he realized that all was lost. He withdrew into the Tower of David, which he offered to hand over to

Raymond with a great sum of treasure in return for his life and the lives of his bodyguard. Raymond accepted the terms and occupied the Tower. Iftikhar and his men were safely escorted out of the city and permitted to join the Moslem garrison of Ascalon.

They were the only Moslems in Jerusalem to save their lives. The Crusaders, maddened by so great a victory after such suffering, rushed through the streets and into the houses and mosques killing all that they met, men, women and children alike. All that afternoon and all through the night the massacre continued. Tancred's banner was no protection to the refugees in the mosque of al-Aqsa. Early next morning a band of Crusaders forced an entry into the mosque and slew everyone. When Raymond of Aguilers later that morning went to visit the Temple area he had to pick his way through corpses and blood that reached up to his knees.

The Jews of Jerusalem fled in a body to their chief synagogue. But they were held to have aided the Moslems; and no mercy was shown to them. The building was set on fire and they were all burnt within.

The massacre at Jerusalem profoundly impressed all the world. No one can say how many victims it involved; but it emptied Jerusalem of its Moslem and Jewish inhabitants. Many even of the Christians were horrified by what had been done; and amongst the Moslems, who had been ready hitherto to accept the Franks as another factor in the tangled politics of the time, there was henceforward a clear determination that the Franks must be driven out. It was this bloodthirsty proof of Christian fanaticism that recreated the fanaticism of Islam. When, later, wiser Latins in the East sought to find some basis on which Christian and Moslem could work together, the memory of the massacre stood always in their way.

When there were no more Moslems left to be slain, the princes of the Crusade went in solemn state through the desolate Christian quarter, deserted since Iftikhar had exiled its inhabitants, to give thanks to God in the Church of the Holy Sepulchre. Then, on 17 July, they met together to appoint a ruler for the conquered city.

The ruler whom most would have welcomed was dead. The whole army grieved that Bishop Adhemar of Le Puy should not be living to see the triumph of the cause that he had served. It was not to be believed that he had not really seen it. Soldier after soldier testified that there had been a warrior fighting in the forefront of the assault, in whom they had recognized the features of the Bishop. Others too, who would have rejoiced in the victory, did not survive to hear of it. Symeon, Patriarch of Jerusalem, had died a few days earlier in exile in Cyprus. Far away in Italy the founder of the Crusade was lying sick. On 29 July 1099, a fortnight after his soldiers had entered the Holy City, but before any news of it could reach him, Pope Urban II died at Rome.

POCKET PENGUINS

POCKET PENGUINS